A SPY IN THE FIELD

MOE BERG'S STORY

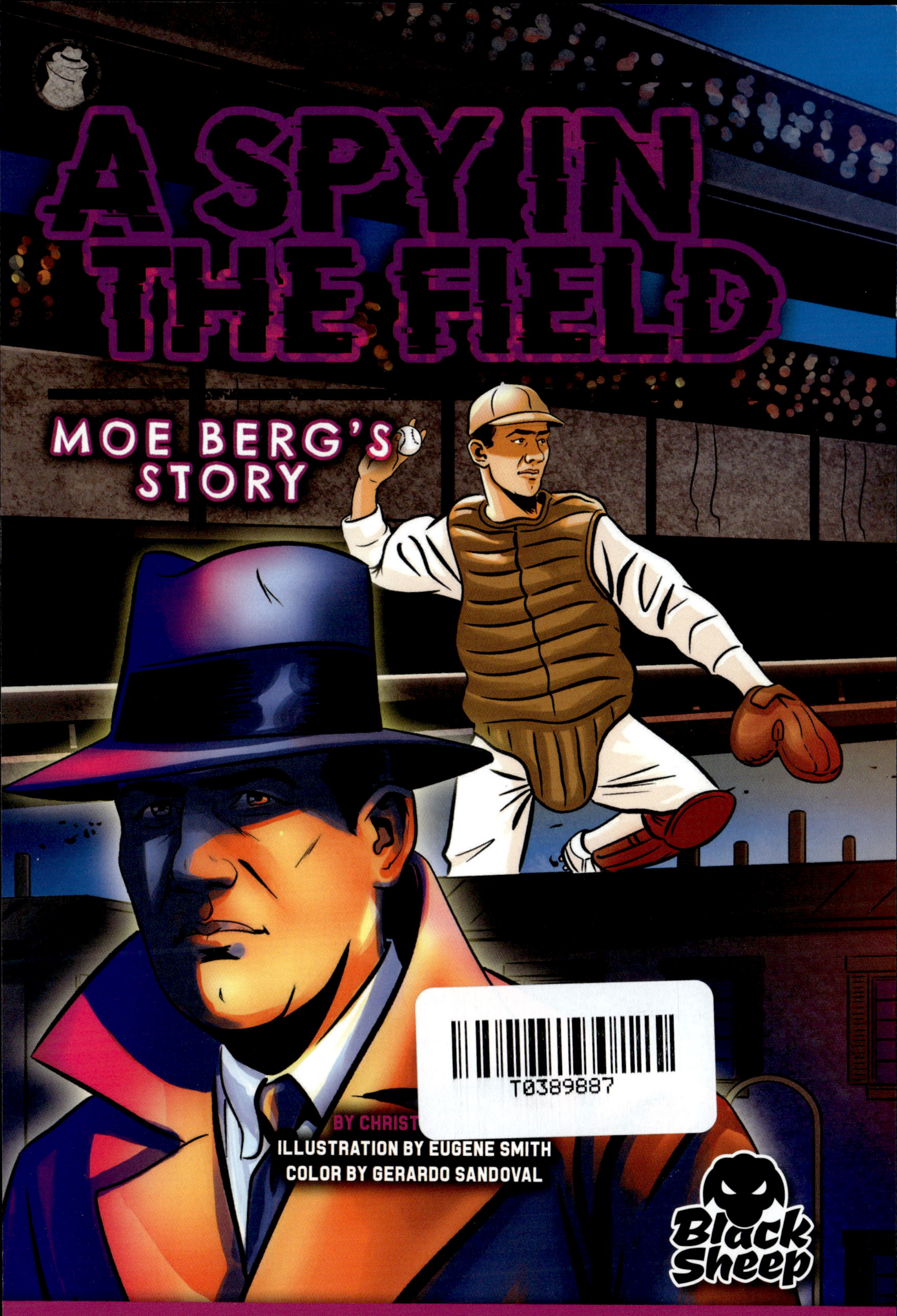

BY CHRIST

ILLUSTRATION BY EUGENE SMITH
COLOR BY GERARDO SANDOVAL

Black Sheep

BELLWETHER MEDIA • MINNEAPOLIS, MN

STRAY FROM REGULAR READS WITH BLACK SHEEP BOOKS. FEEL A RUSH WITH EVERY READ!

This edition first published in 2025 by Bellwether Media, Inc.

No part of this publication may be reproduced in whole or in part without written permission of the publisher. For information regarding permission, write to Bellwether Media, Inc., Attention: Permissions Department, 6012 Blue Circle Drive, Minnetonka, MN 55343.

Library of Congress Cataloging-in-Publication Data

Names: Leaf, Christina, author. | Smith, Eugene (Illustrator), illustrator.
Title: A spy in the field : Moe Berg's story / by Christina Leaf ; [illustrated by] Eugene Smith.
Other titles: Moe Berg's story
Description: Minneapolis, MN : Bellwether Media, Inc., 2025. | Series: Black Sheep : Top secret spy stories | Includes bibliographical references and index. | Audience: Ages 7-13 | Audience: Grades 4-6 | Summary: "Exciting illustrations follow the events of Moe Berg's spying career. The combination of brightly colored panels and leveled text is intended for students in grades 3 through 8"– Provided by publisher.
Identifiers: LCCN 2024021924 (print) | LCCN 2024021925 (ebook) | ISBN 9798893040616 (library binding) | ISBN 9798893041682 (paperback) | ISBN 9781648348914 (ebook)
Subjects: LCSH: Berg, Moe, 1902-1972–Juvenile literature. | World War, 1939-1945–Secret service–United States–Juvenile literature. | Spies–United States–Biography–Juvenile literature. | Baseball players–United States–Biography–Juvenile literature. | United States. Office of Strategic Services–Biography–Juvenile literature. | Berg, Moe, 1902-1972–Comic books, strips, etc. | World War, 1939-1945–Secret service–United States–Comic books, strips, etc. | Spies–United States–Biography–Comic books, strips, etc. | United States. Office of Strategic Services–Biography–Juvenile literature. | Baseball players–United States–Biography–Comic books, strips, etc.
Classification: LCC D810.S8 B4695 2025 (print) | LCC D810.S8 (ebook) | DDC 940.54/8673 [B]–dc23/eng/20240514
LC record available at https://lccn.loc.gov/2024021924
LC ebook record available at https://lccn.loc.gov/2024021925

Text copyright © 2025 by Bellwether Media, Inc. BLACK SHEEP and associated logos are trademarks and/or registered trademarks of Bellwether Media, Inc. Bellwether Media is a division of Chrysalis Education Group.

Editor: Kieran Downs   Designer: Andrea Schneider

Printed in the United States of America, North Mankato, MN.

TABLE OF CONTENTS

A COVERT CATCHER	4
IN THE FIELD	10
CATCHING HEISENBERG	14
MORE ABOUT MOE BERG	22
GLOSSARY	23
TO LEARN MORE	24
INDEX	24

Red text identifies historical quotes.

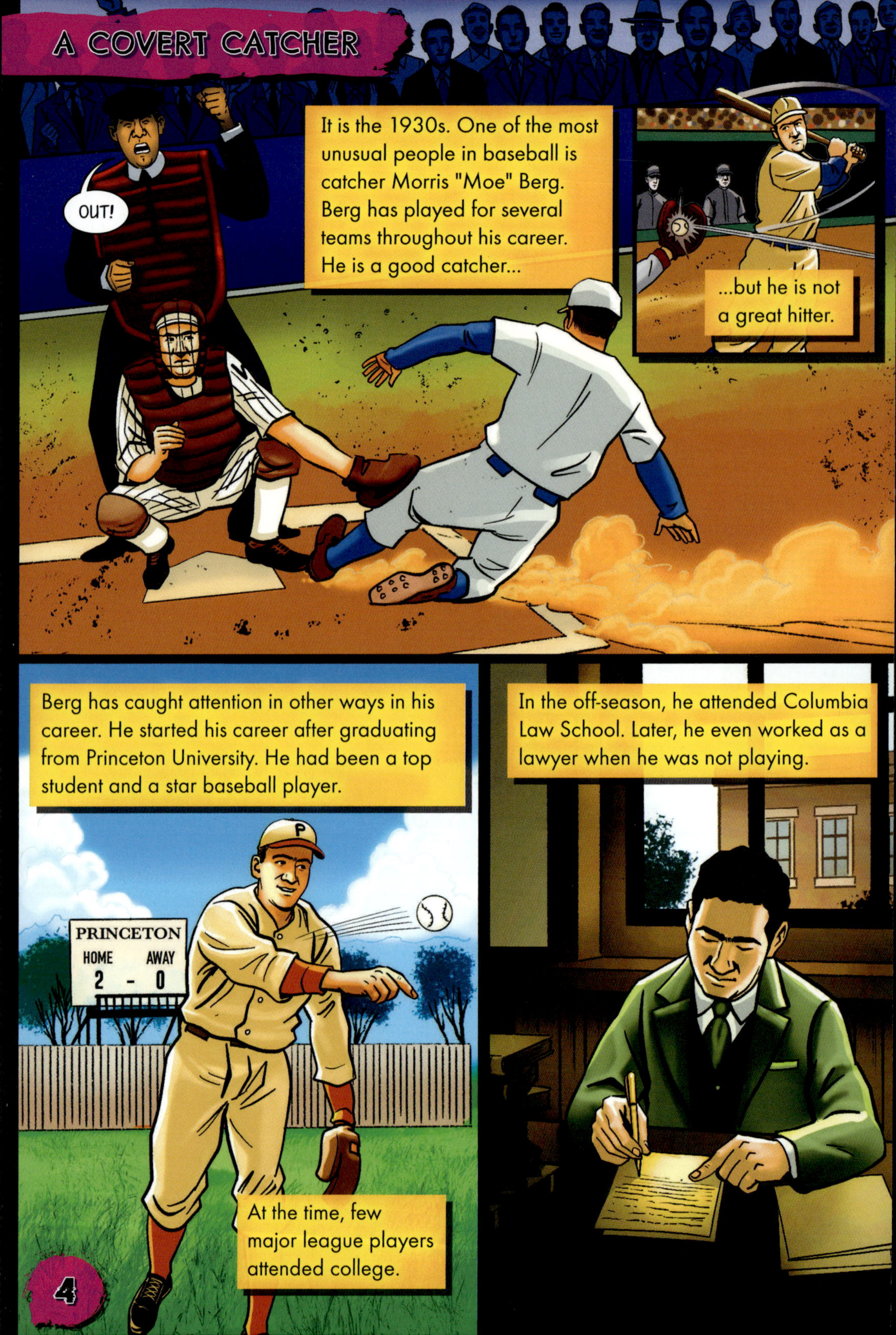

A COVERT CATCHER
OUT!
It is the 1930s. One of the most unusual people in baseball is catcher Morris "Moe" Berg. Berg has played for several teams throughout his career. He is a good catcher...
...but he is not a great hitter.
Berg has caught attention in other ways in his career. He started his career after graduating from Princeton University. He had been a top student and a star baseball player.
PRINCETON
HOME AWAY
2 - 0
At the time, few major league players attended college.
In the off-season, he attended Columbia Law School. Later, he even worked as a lawyer when he was not playing.

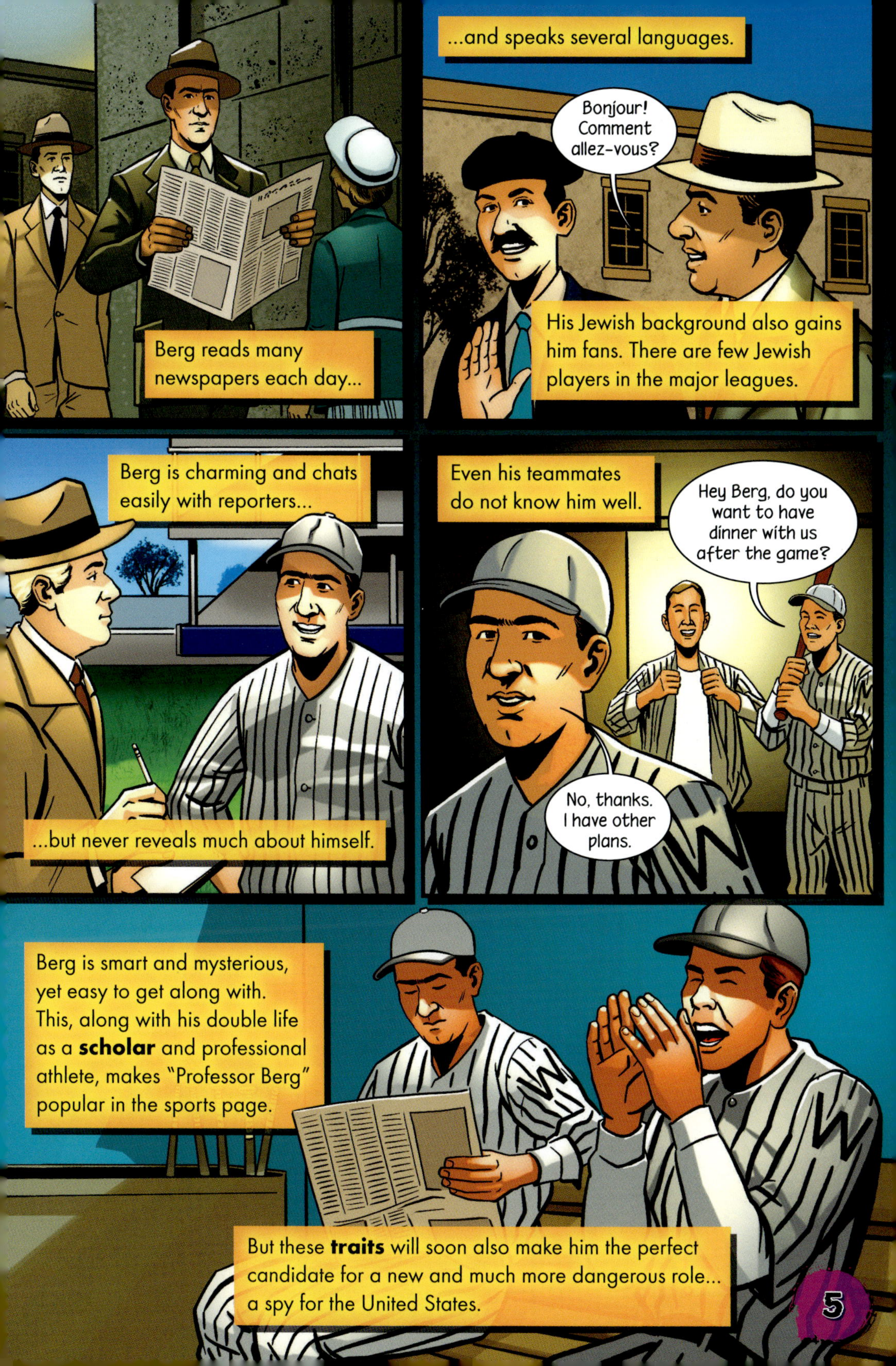
Berg reads many newspapers each day...
...and speaks several languages.
Bonjour! Comment allez-vous?
His Jewish background also gains him fans. There are few Jewish players in the major leagues.
Berg is charming and chats easily with reporters...
...but never reveals much about himself.
Even his teammates do not know him well.
Hey Berg, do you want to have dinner with us after the game?
No, thanks. I have other plans.
Berg is smart and mysterious, yet easy to get along with. This, along with his double life as a **scholar** and professional athlete, makes "Professor Berg" popular in the sports page.
But these **traits** will soon also make him the perfect candidate for a new and much more dangerous role... a spy for the United States.

It is 1934. Many of America's top baseball players, including Babe Ruth and Lou Gehrig, have agreed to an **exhibition** tour in Japan. Berg made a similar trip two years earlier. Due to his popularity on the previous trip, Berg is asked to join.

The Americans will travel across Japan, taking on a team of Japanese all-stars.

Do you speak Japanese?

I never had occasion to learn it.

An eager student, Berg spends the trip across the ocean studying Japanese.

By the time they reach Japan, Berg knows enough Japanese to speak with locals.

«We're happy to be here!»

You told me you didn't speak Japanese.

That was two weeks ago.

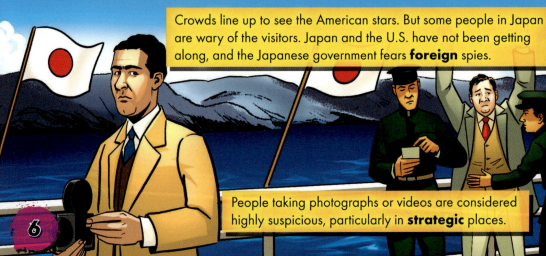

Crowds line up to see the American stars. But some people in Japan are wary of the visitors. Japan and the U.S. have not been getting along, and the Japanese government fears **foreign** spies.

People taking photographs or videos are considered highly suspicious, particularly in **strategic** places.

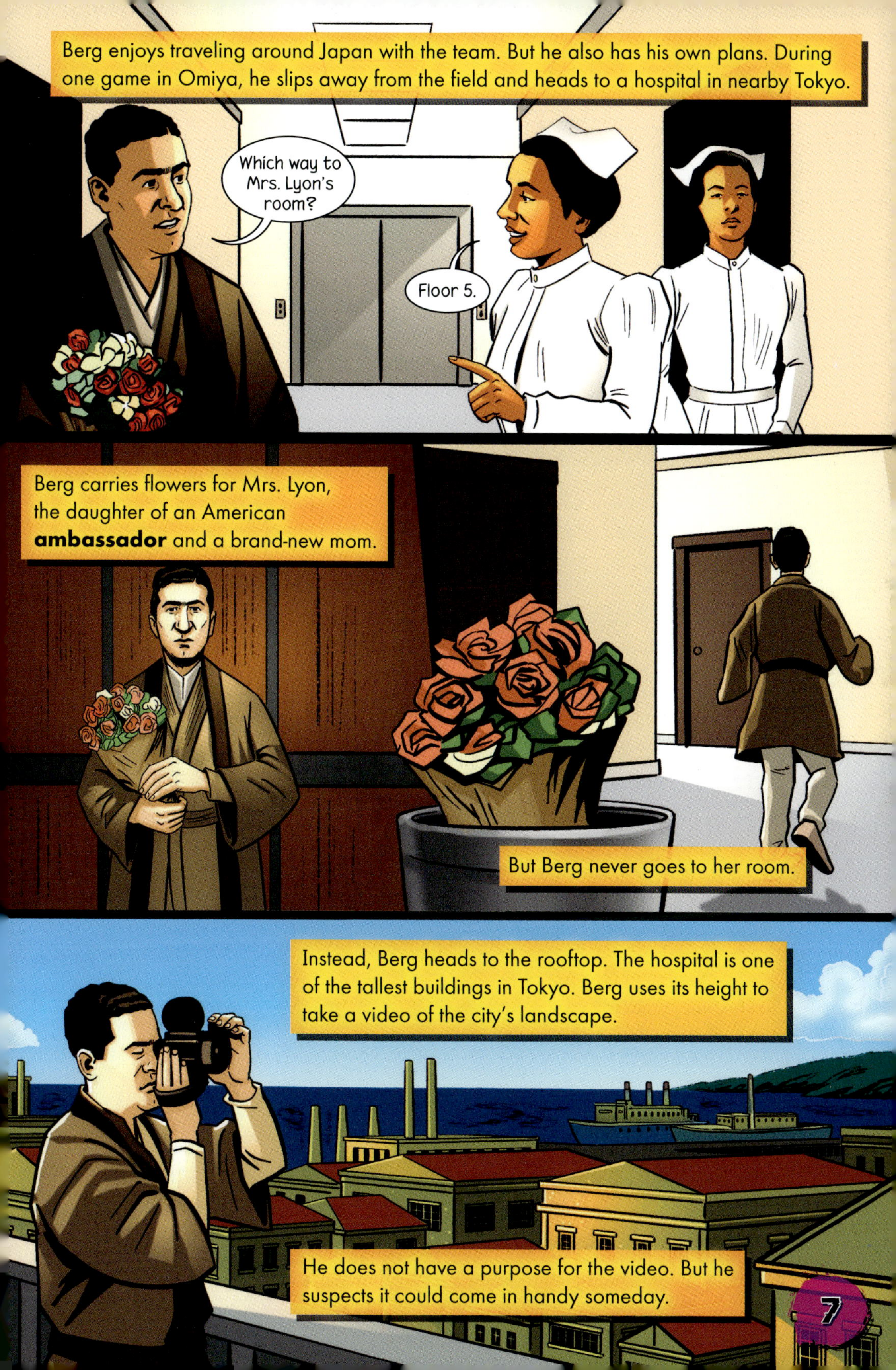
Berg enjoys traveling around Japan with the team. But he also has his own plans. During one game in Omiya, he slips away from the field and heads to a hospital in nearby Tokyo.
Which way to Mrs. Lyon's room?
Floor 5.
Berg carries flowers for Mrs. Lyon, the daughter of an American **ambassador** and a brand-new mom.
But Berg never goes to her room.
Instead, Berg heads to the rooftop. The hospital is one of the tallest buildings in Tokyo. Berg uses its height to take a video of the city's landscape.
He does not have a purpose for the video. But he suspects it could come in handy someday.

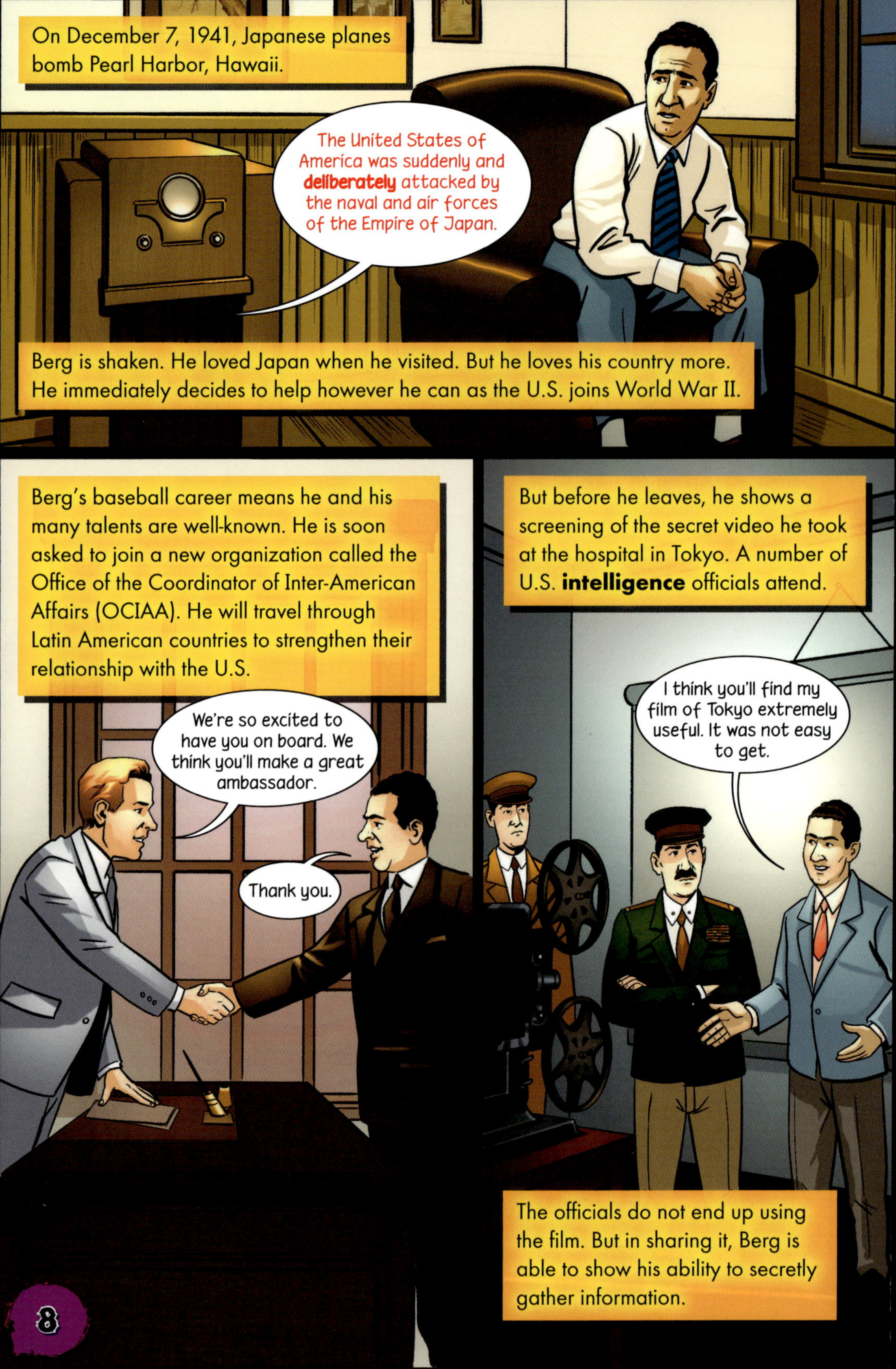
On December 7, 1941, Japanese planes bomb Pearl Harbor, Hawaii.
The United States of America was suddenly and **deliberately** attacked by the naval and air forces of the Empire of Japan.
Berg is shaken. He loved Japan when he visited. But he loves his country more. He immediately decides to help however he can as the U.S. joins World War II.
Berg's baseball career means he and his many talents are well-known. He is soon asked to join a new organization called the Office of the Coordinator of Inter-American Affairs (OCIAA). He will travel through Latin American countries to strengthen their relationship with the U.S.
We're so excited to have you on board. We think you'll make a great ambassador.
Thank you.
But before he leaves, he shows a screening of the secret video he took at the hospital in Tokyo. A number of U.S. **intelligence** officials attend.
I think you'll find my film of Tokyo extremely useful. It was not easy to get.
The officials do not end up using the film. But in sharing it, Berg is able to show his ability to secretly gather information.

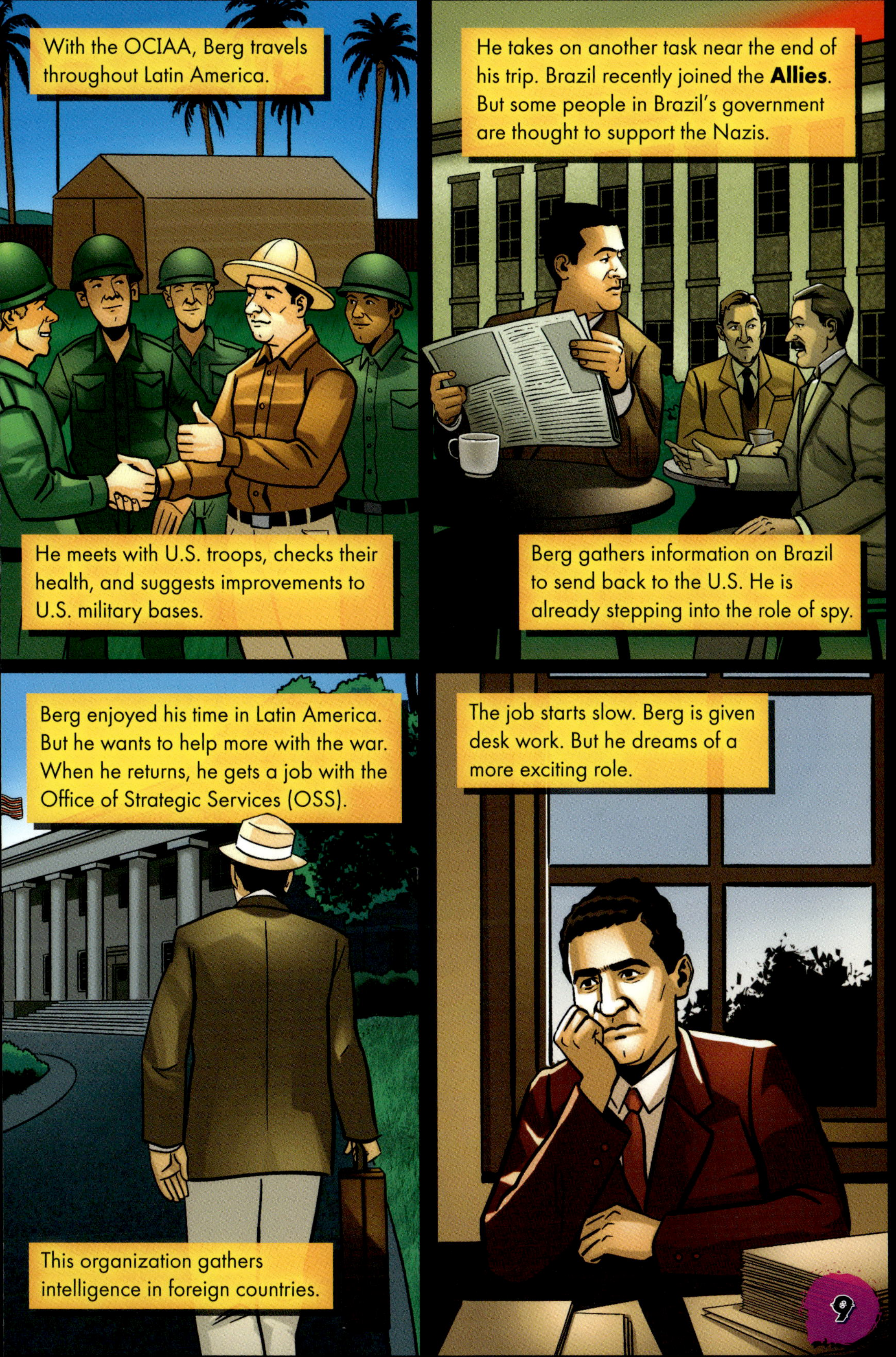
With the OCIAA, Berg travels throughout Latin America.
He meets with U.S. troops, checks their health, and suggests improvements to U.S. military bases.
He takes on another task near the end of his trip. Brazil recently joined the **Allies**. But some people in Brazil's government are thought to support the Nazis.
Berg gathers information on Brazil to send back to the U.S. He is already stepping into the role of spy.
Berg enjoyed his time in Latin America. But he wants to help more with the war. When he returns, he gets a job with the Office of Strategic Services (OSS).
This organization gathers intelligence in foreign countries.
The job starts slow. Berg is given desk work. But he dreams of a more exciting role.

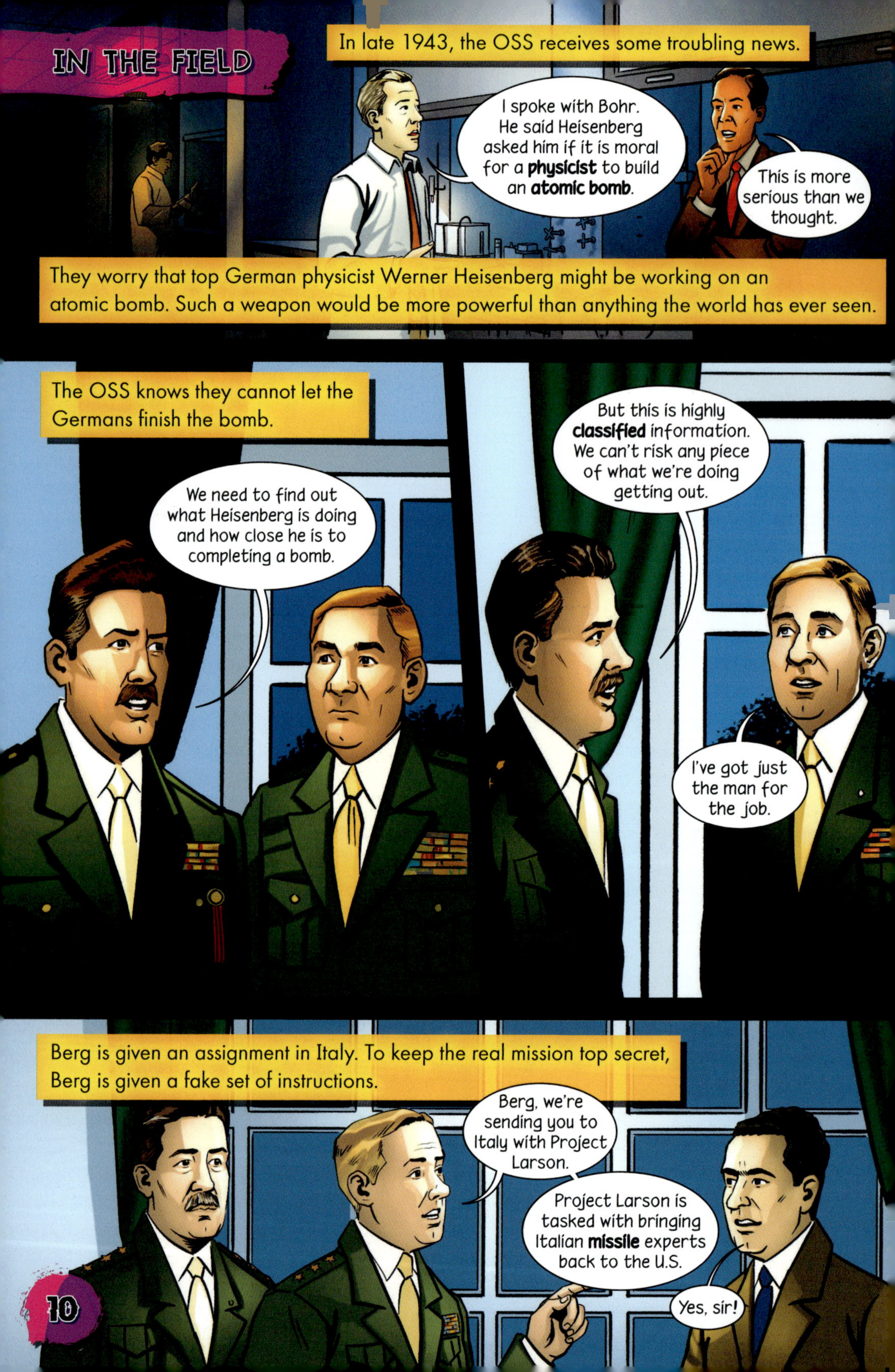
In late 1943, the OSS receives some troubling news.
I spoke with Bohr. He said Heisenberg asked him if it is moral for a **physicist** to build an **atomic bomb**.
This is more serious than we thought.
They worry that top German physicist Werner Heisenberg might be working on an atomic bomb. Such a weapon would be more powerful than anything the world has ever seen.
The OSS knows they cannot let the Germans finish the bomb.
We need to find out what Heisenberg is doing and how close he is to completing a bomb.
But this is highly **classified** information. We can't risk any piece of what we're doing getting out.
I've got just the man for the job.
Berg is given an assignment in Italy. To keep the real mission top secret, Berg is given a fake set of instructions.
Berg, we're sending you to Italy with Project Larson.
Project Larson is tasked with bringing Italian **missile** experts back to the U.S.
Yes, sir!

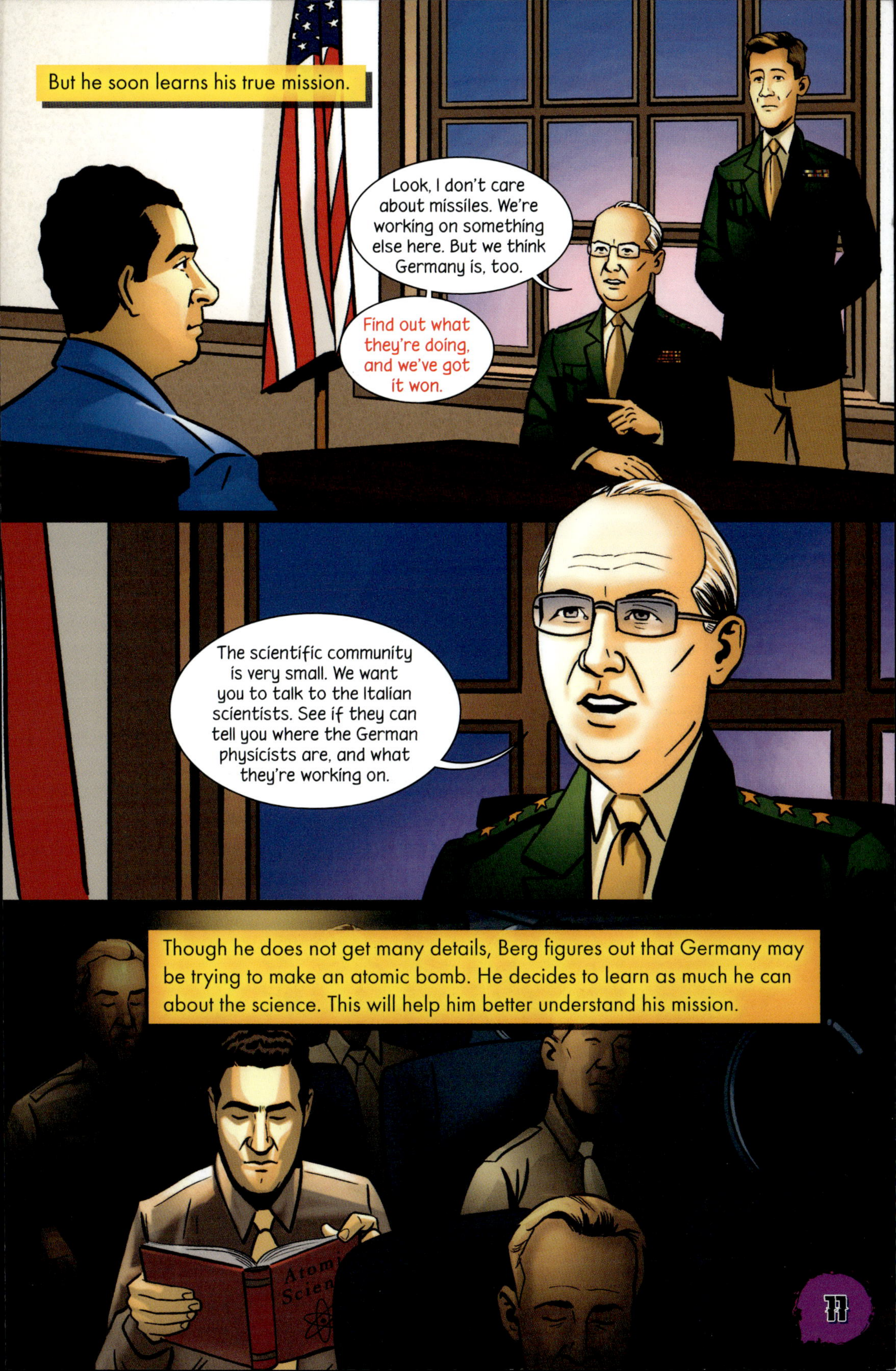
But he soon learns his true mission.
Look, I don't care about missiles. We're working on something else here. But we think Germany is, too.
Find out what they're doing, and we've got it won.
The scientific community is very small. We want you to talk to the Italian scientists. See if they can tell you where the German physicists are, and what they're working on.
Though he does not get many details, Berg figures out that Germany may be trying to make an atomic bomb. He decides to learn as much he can about the science. This will help him better understand his mission.

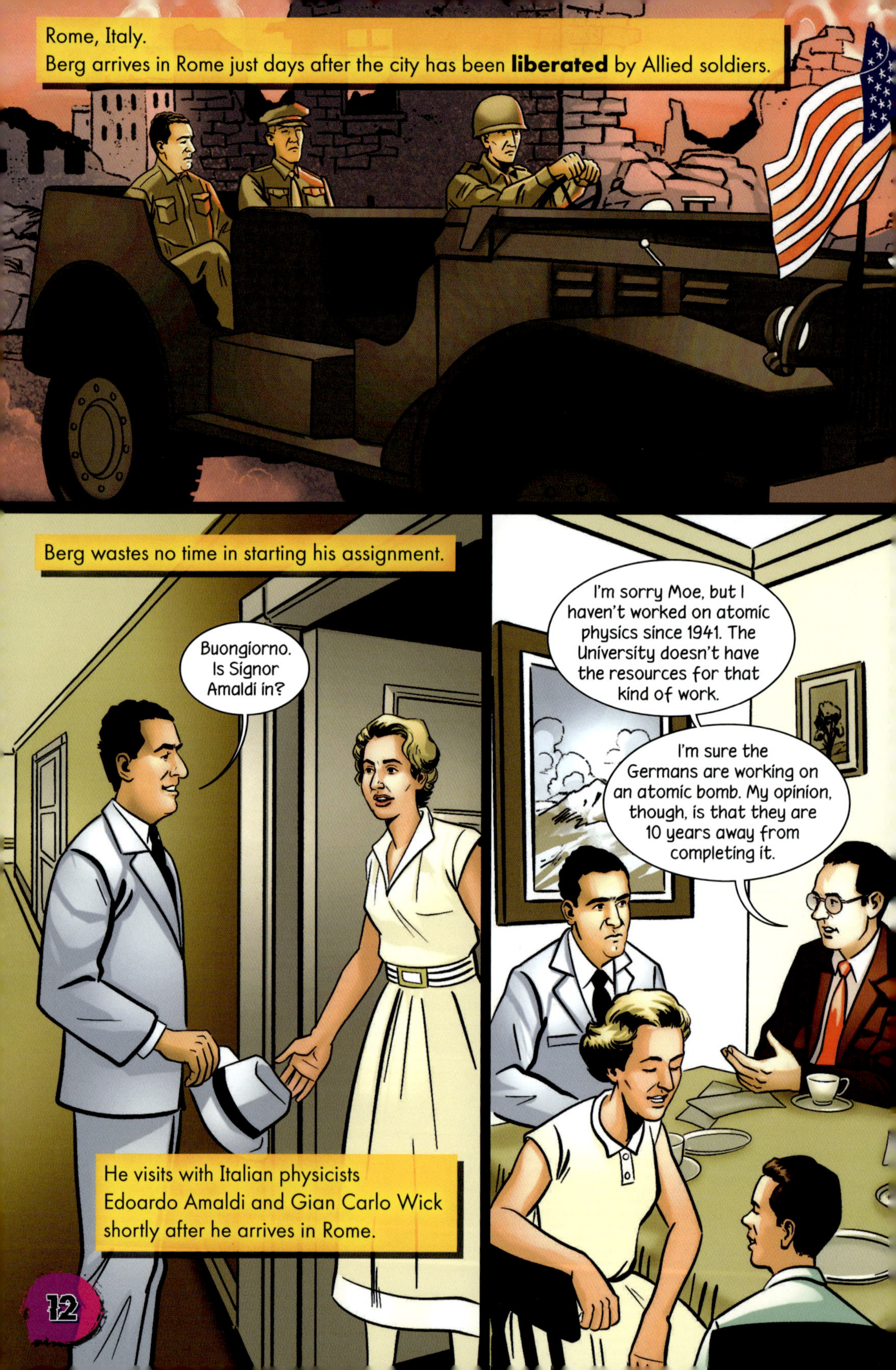
Rome, Italy.
Berg arrives in Rome just days after the city has been **liberated** by Allied soldiers.
Berg wastes no time in starting his assignment.
Buongiorno. Is Signor Amaldi in?
He visits with Italian physicists Edoardo Amaldi and Gian Carlo Wick shortly after he arrives in Rome.
I'm sorry Moe, but I haven't worked on atomic physics since 1941. The University doesn't have the resources for that kind of work.
I'm sure the Germans are working on an atomic bomb. My opinion, though, is that they are 10 years away from completing it.

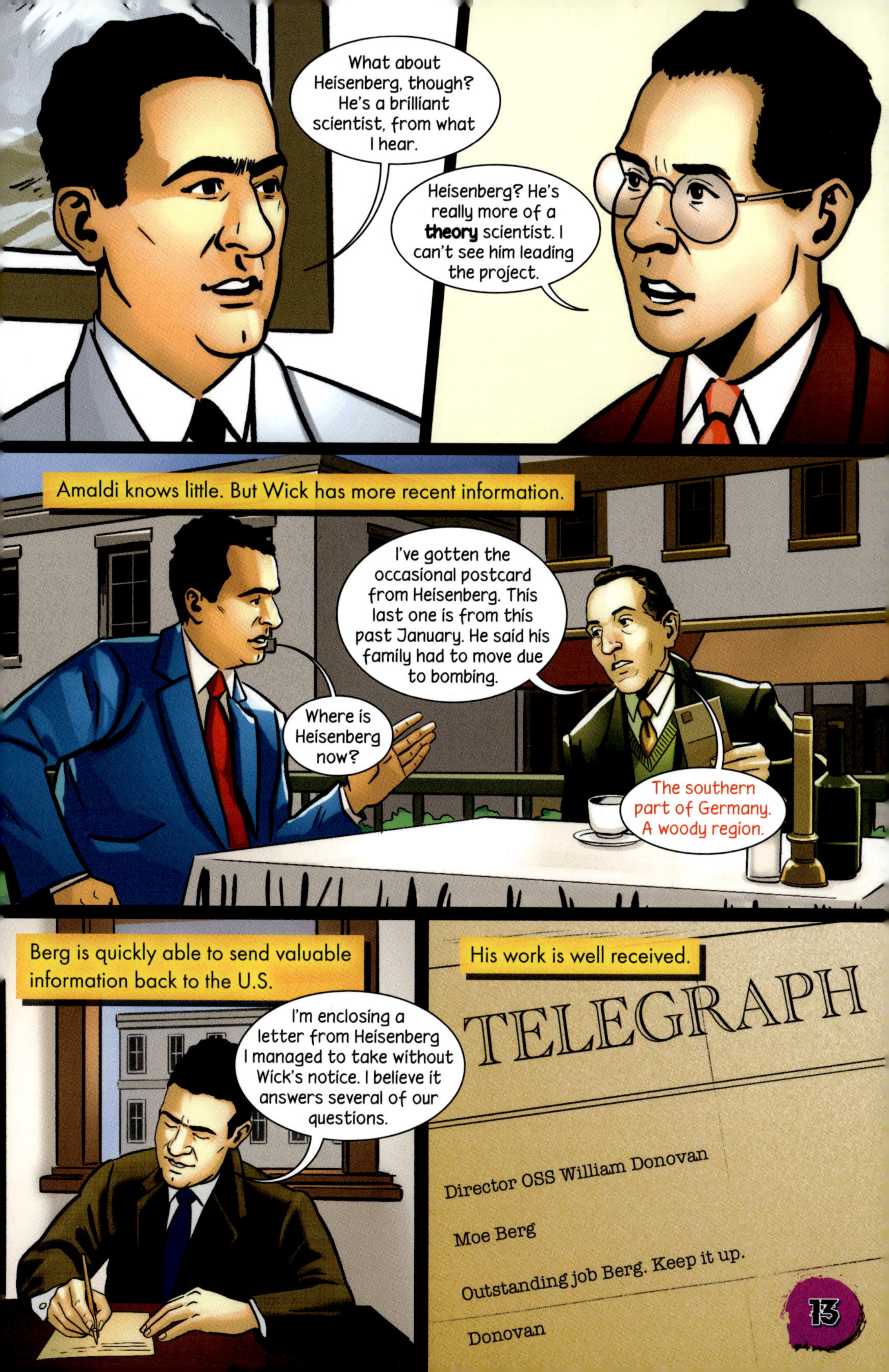
What about Heisenberg, though? He's a brilliant scientist, from what I hear.
Heisenberg? He's really more of a **theory** scientist. I can't see him leading the project.
Amaldi knows little. But Wick has more recent information.
Where is Heisenberg now?
I've gotten the occasional postcard from Heisenberg. This last one is from this past January. He said his family had to move due to bombing.
The southern part of Germany. A woody region.
Berg is quickly able to send valuable information back to the U.S.
I'm enclosing a letter from Heisenberg I managed to take without Wick's notice. I believe it answers several of our questions.
His work is well received.
TELEGRAPH
Director OSS William Donovan
Moe Berg
Outstanding job Berg. Keep it up.
Donovan

CATCHING HEISENBERG

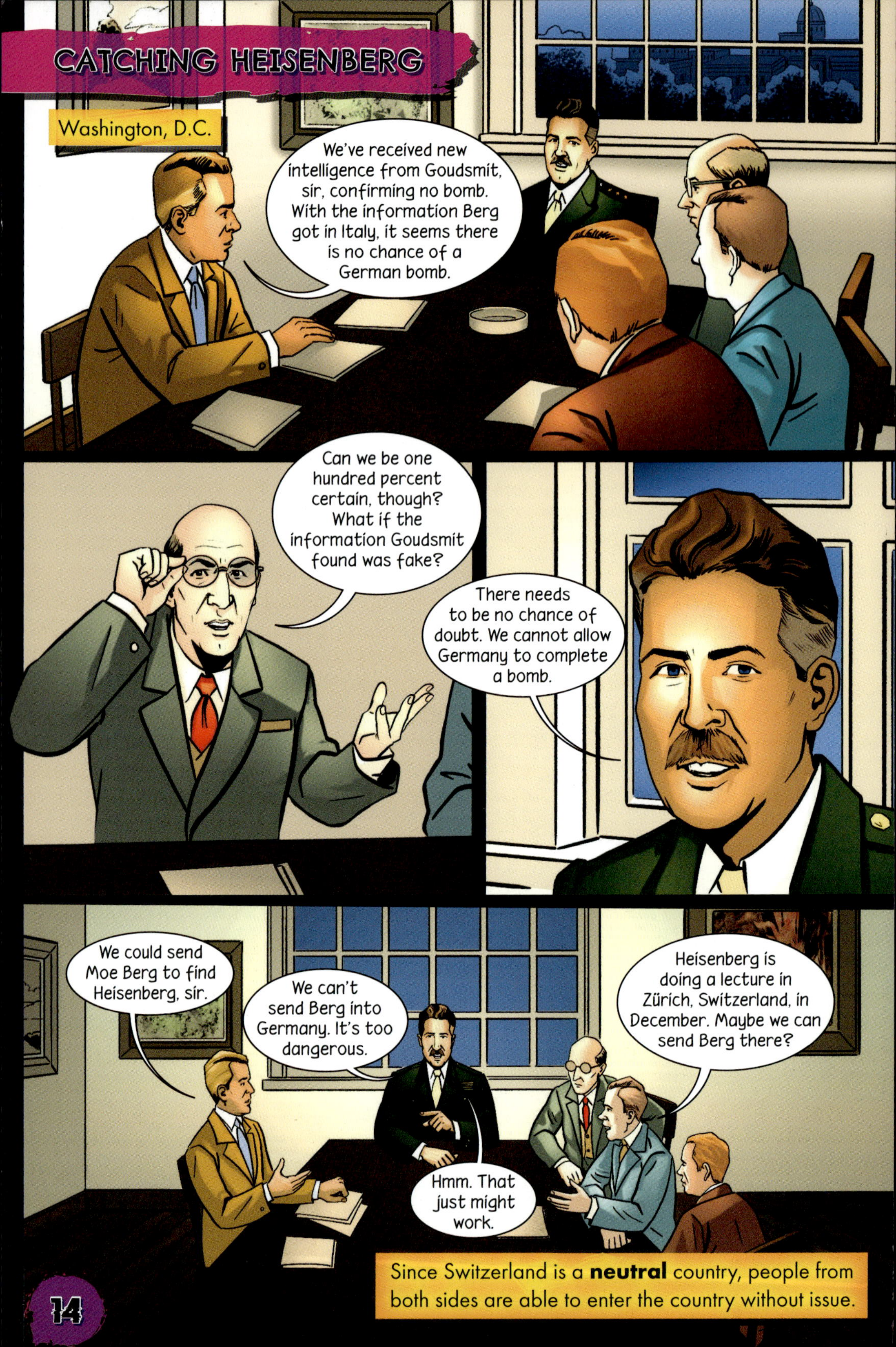
Washington, D.C.
We've received new intelligence from Goudsmit, sir, confirming no bomb. With the information Berg got in Italy, it seems there is no chance of a German bomb.
Can we be one hundred percent certain, though? What if the information Goudsmit found was fake?
There needs to be no chance of doubt. We cannot allow Germany to complete a bomb.
We could send Moe Berg to find Heisenberg, sir.
We can't send Berg into Germany. It's too dangerous.
Heisenberg is doing a lecture in Zürich, Switzerland, in December. Maybe we can send Berg there?
Hmm. That just might work.
Since Switzerland is a **neutral** country, people from both sides are able to enter the country without issue.

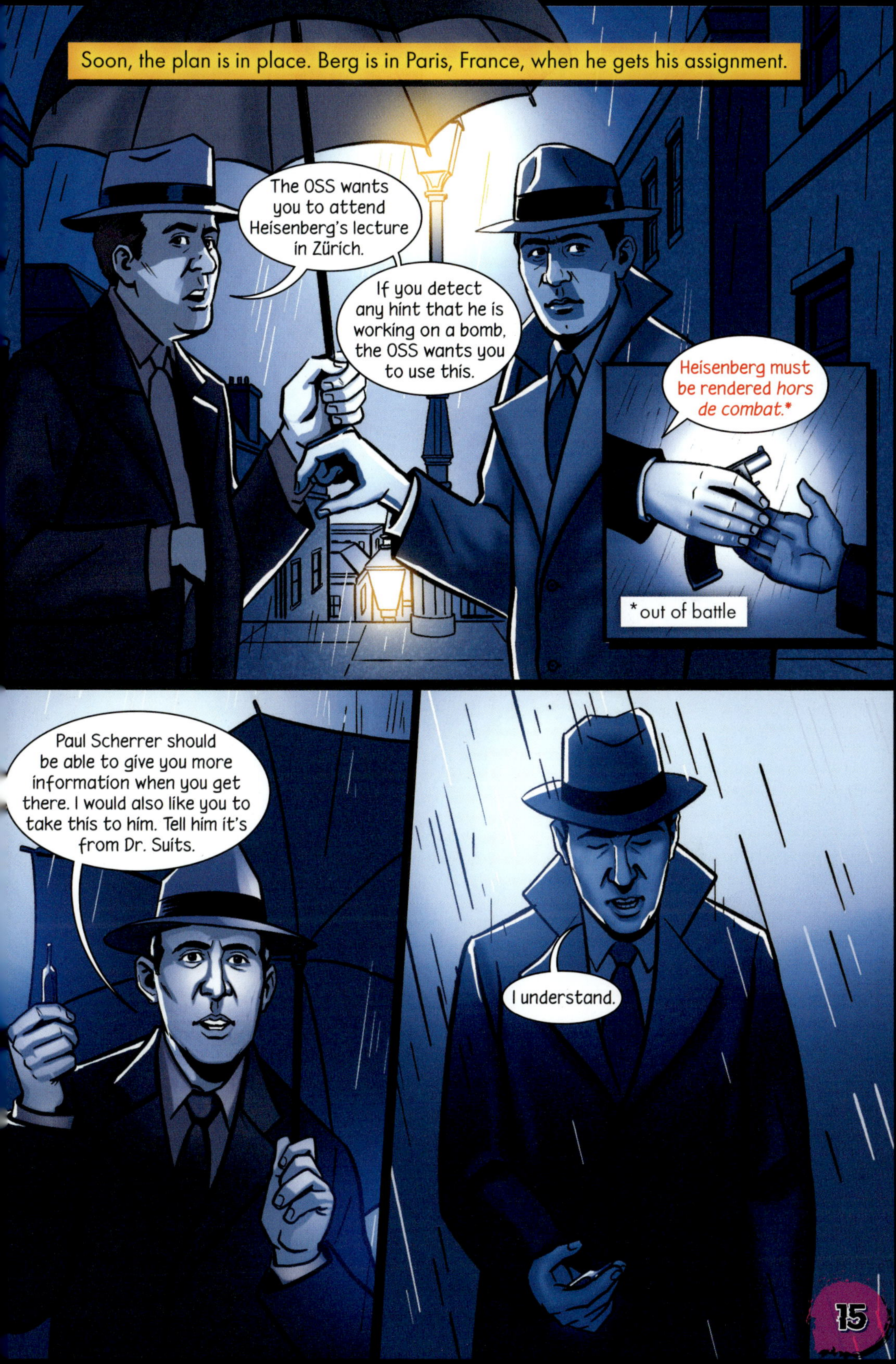
Soon, the plan is in place. Berg is in Paris, France, when he gets his assignment.
The OSS wants you to attend Heisenberg's lecture in Zürich.
If you detect any hint that he is working on a bomb, the OSS wants you to use this.
Heisenberg must be rendered *hors de combat.**
*out of battle
Paul Scherrer should be able to give you more information when you get there. I would also like you to take this to him. Tell him it's from Dr. Suits.
I understand.

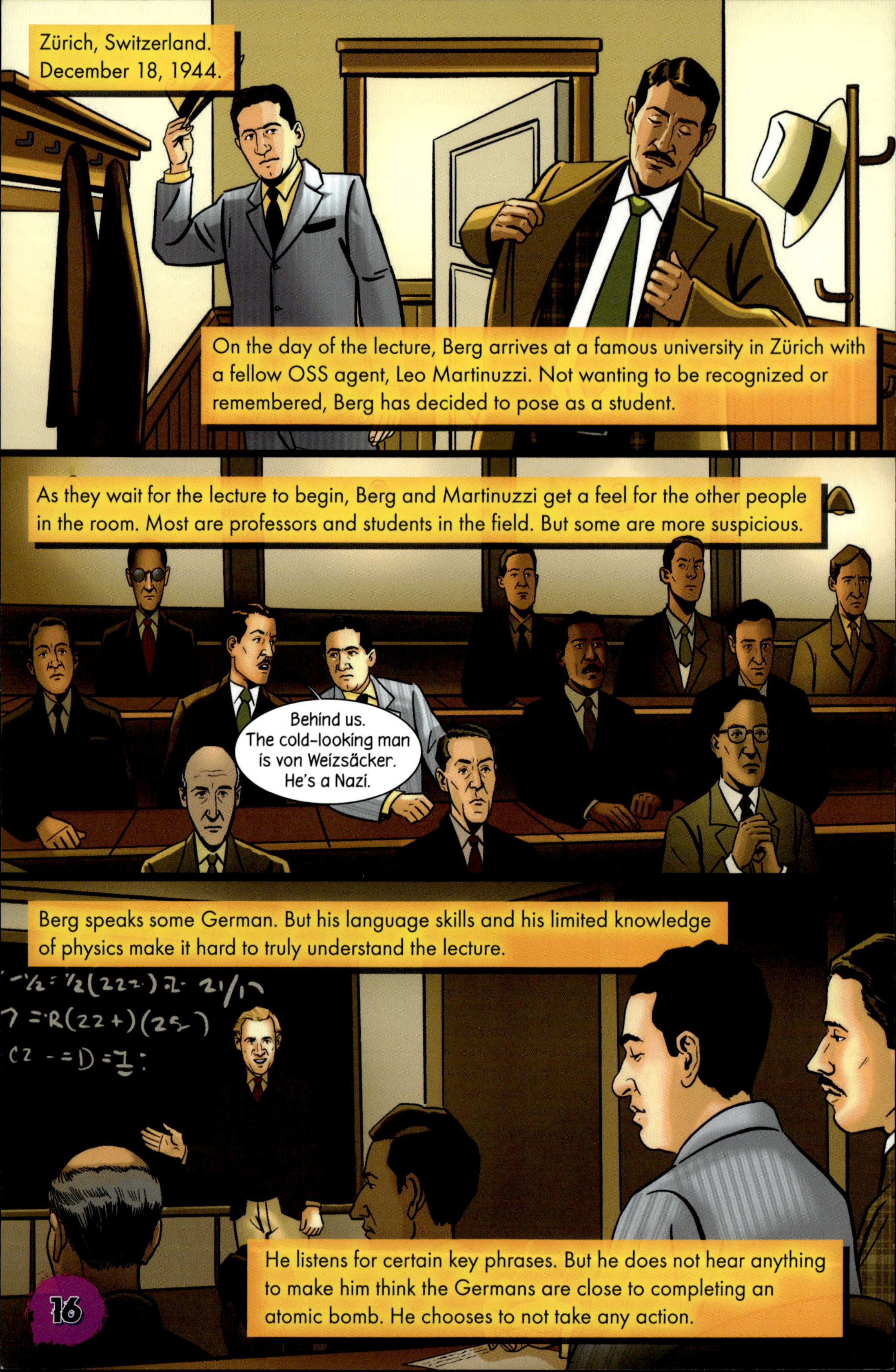
Zürich, Switzerland.
December 18, 1944.
On the day of the lecture, Berg arrives at a famous university in Zürich with a fellow OSS agent, Leo Martinuzzi. Not wanting to be recognized or remembered, Berg has decided to pose as a student.
As they wait for the lecture to begin, Berg and Martinuzzi get a feel for the other people in the room. Most are professors and students in the field. But some are more suspicious.
Behind us. The cold-looking man is von Weizsäcker. He's a Nazi.
Berg speaks some German. But his language skills and his limited knowledge of physics make it hard to truly understand the lecture.
He listens for certain key phrases. But he does not hear anything to make him think the Germans are close to completing an atomic bomb. He chooses to not take any action.

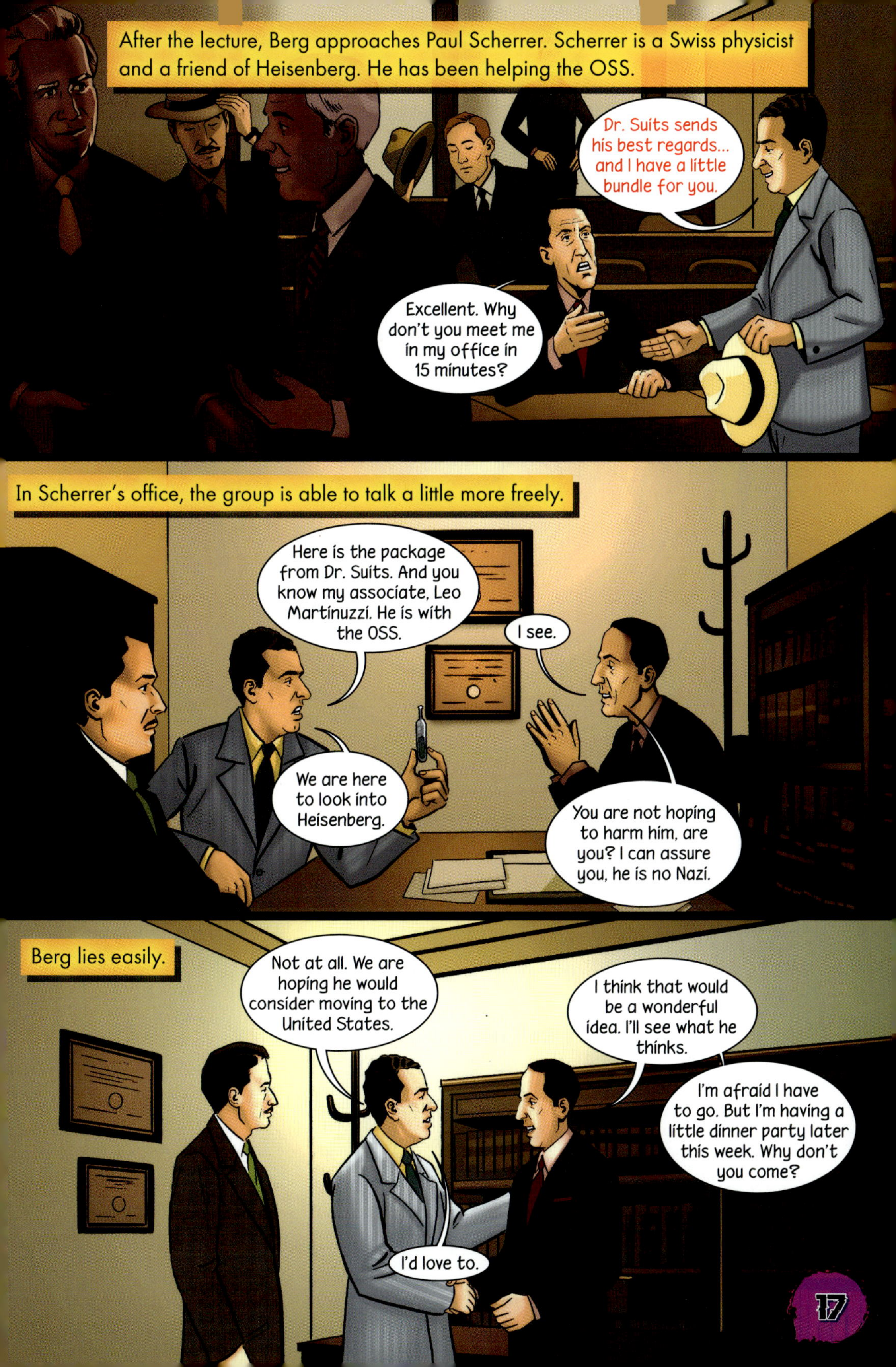
After the lecture, Berg approaches Paul Scherrer. Scherrer is a Swiss physicist and a friend of Heisenberg. He has been helping the OSS.
Dr. Suits sends his best regards... and I have a little bundle for you.
Excellent. Why don't you meet me in my office in 15 minutes?
In Scherrer's office, the group is able to talk a little more freely.
Here is the package from Dr. Suits. And you know my associate, Leo Martinuzzi. He is with the OSS.
I see.
We are here to look into Heisenberg.
You are not hoping to harm him, are you? I can assure you, he is no Nazi.
Berg lies easily.
Not at all. We are hoping he would consider moving to the United States.
I think that would be a wonderful idea. I'll see what he thinks.
I'm afraid I have to go. But I'm having a little dinner party later this week. Why don't you come?
I'd love to.

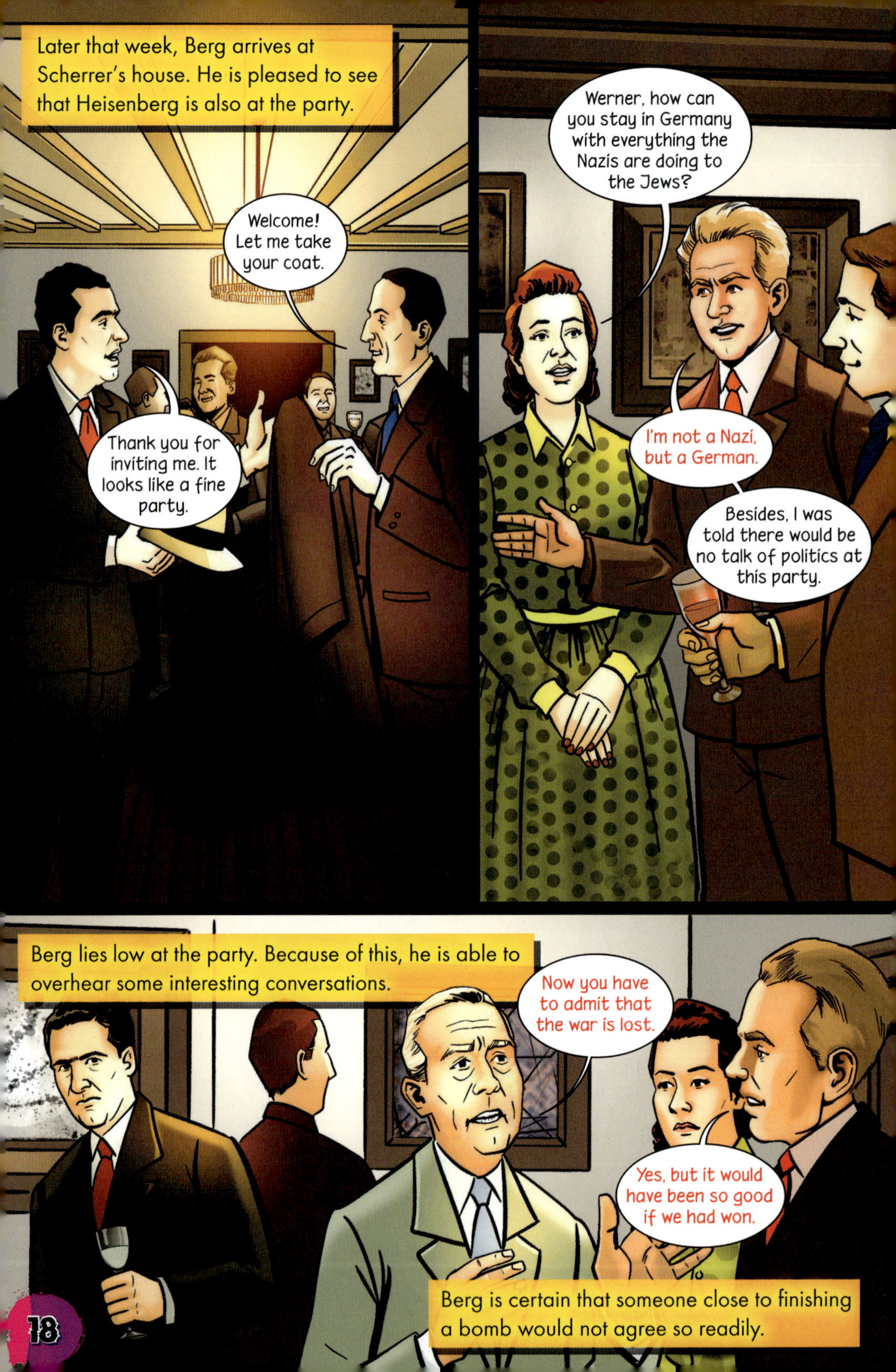
Later that week, Berg arrives at Scherrer's house. He is pleased to see that Heisenberg is also at the party.
Welcome! Let me take your coat.
Thank you for inviting me. It looks like a fine party.
Werner, how can you stay in Germany with everything the Nazis are doing to the Jews?
I'm not a Nazi, but a German.
Besides, I was told there would be no talk of politics at this party.
Berg lies low at the party. Because of this, he is able to overhear some interesting conversations.
Now you have to admit that the war is lost.
Yes, but it would have been so good if we won.
Berg is certain that someone close to finishing a bomb would not agree so readily.

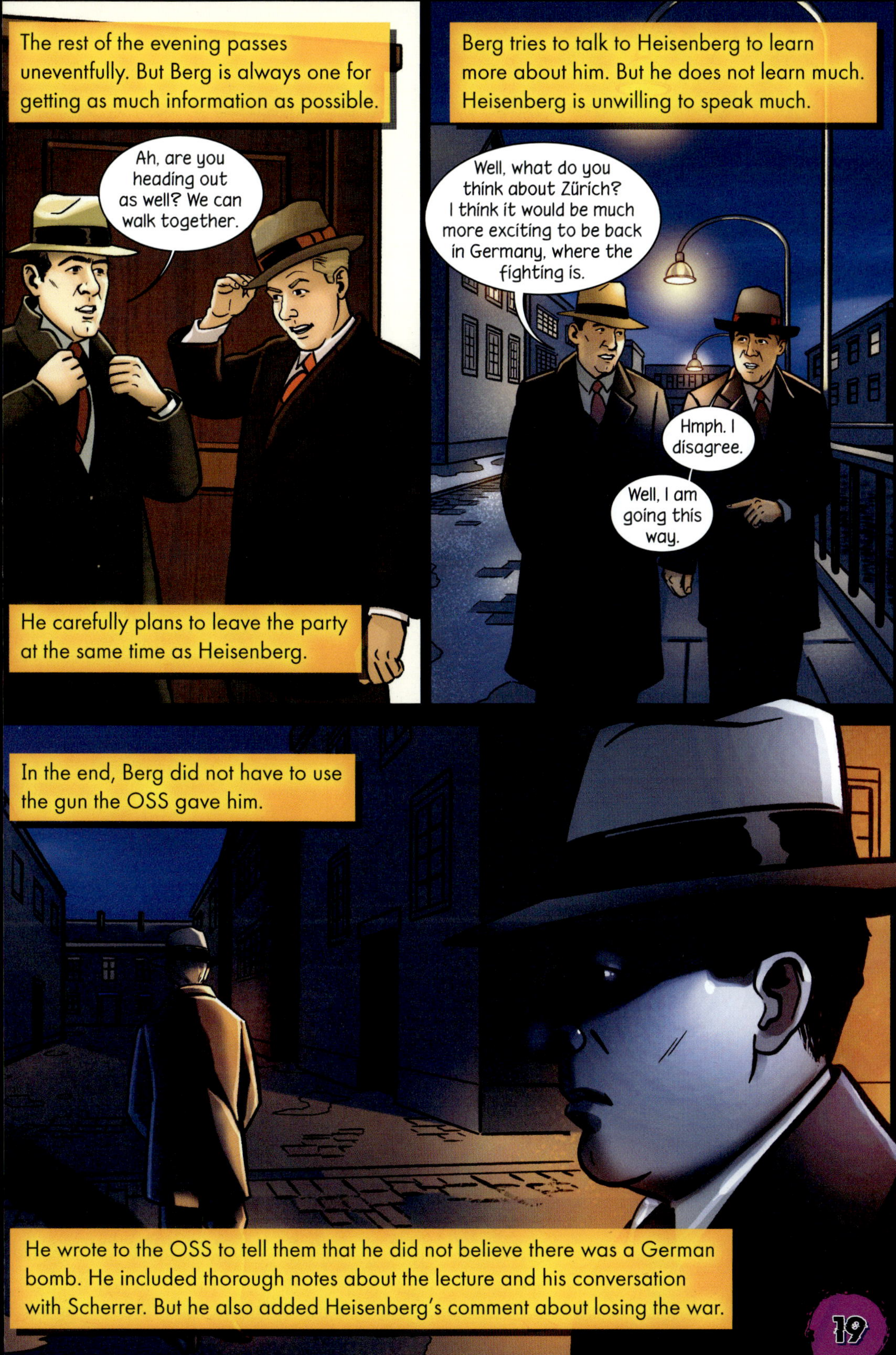
The rest of the evening passes uneventfully. But Berg is always one for getting as much information as possible.
Ah, are you heading out as well? We can walk together.
He carefully plans to leave the party at the same time as Heisenberg.
Berg tries to talk to Heisenberg to learn more about him. But he does not learn much. Heisenberg is unwilling to speak much.
Well, what do you think about Zürich? I think it would be much more exciting to be back in Germany, where the fighting is.
Hmph. I disagree.
Well, I am going this way.
In the end, Berg did not have to use the gun the OSS gave him.
He wrote to the OSS to tell them that he did not believe there was a German bomb. He included thorough notes about the lecture and his conversation with Scherrer. But he also added Heisenberg's comment about losing the war.

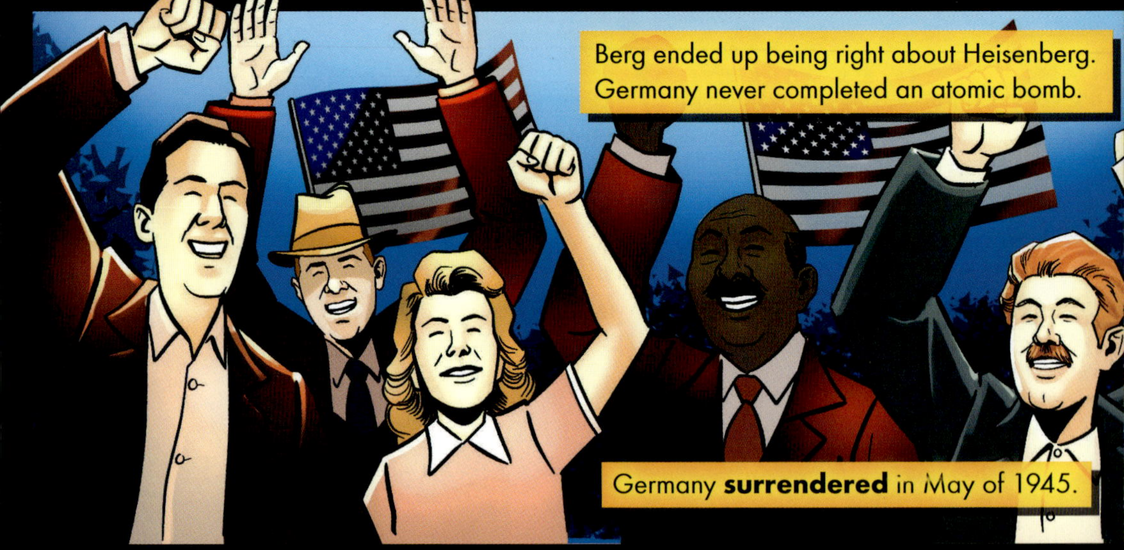
Berg ended up being right about Heisenberg. Germany never completed an atomic bomb.
Germany **surrendered** in May of 1945.

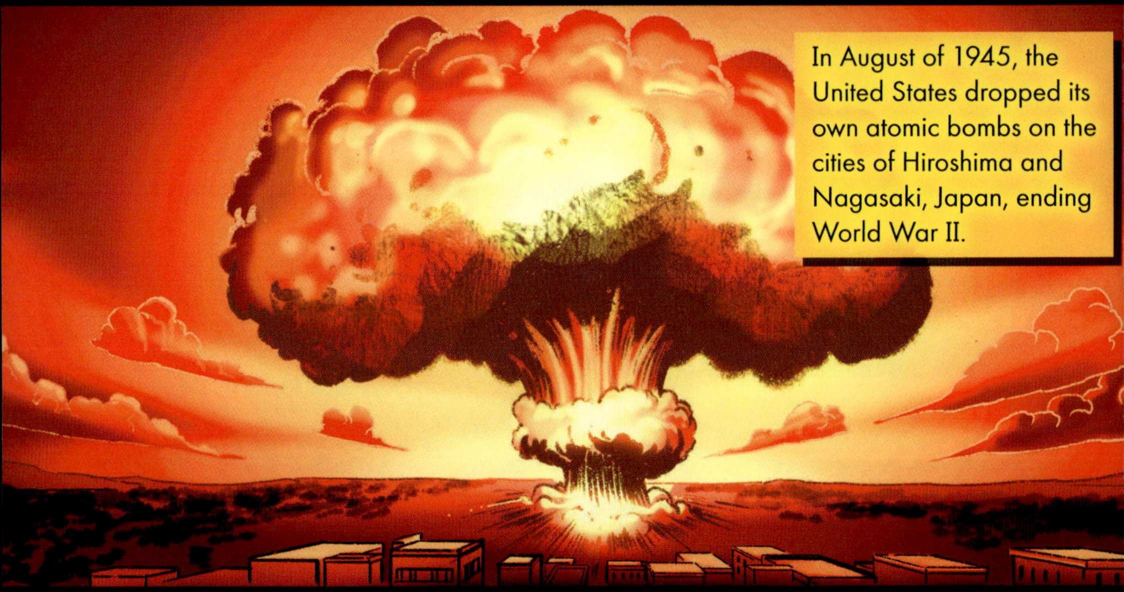
In August of 1945, the United States dropped its own atomic bombs on the cities of Hiroshima and Nagasaki, Japan, ending World War II.

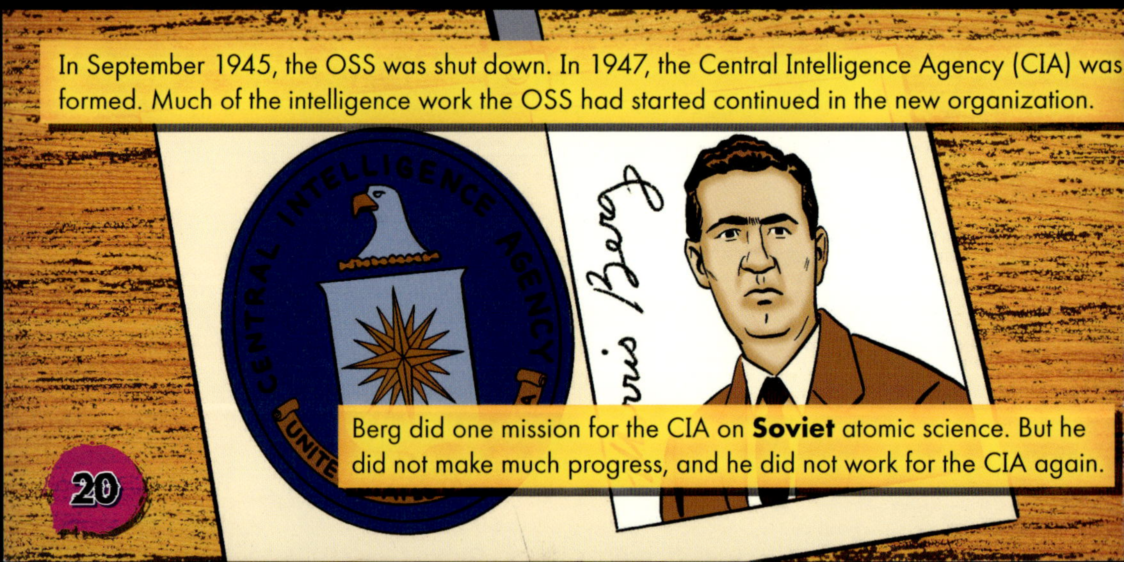
In September 1945, the OSS was shut down. In 1947, the Central Intelligence Agency (CIA) was formed. Much of the intelligence work the OSS had started continued in the new organization.
CENTRAL INTELLIGENCE AGENCY
Berg did one mission for the CIA on **Soviet** atomic science. But he did not make much progress, and he did not work for the CIA again.

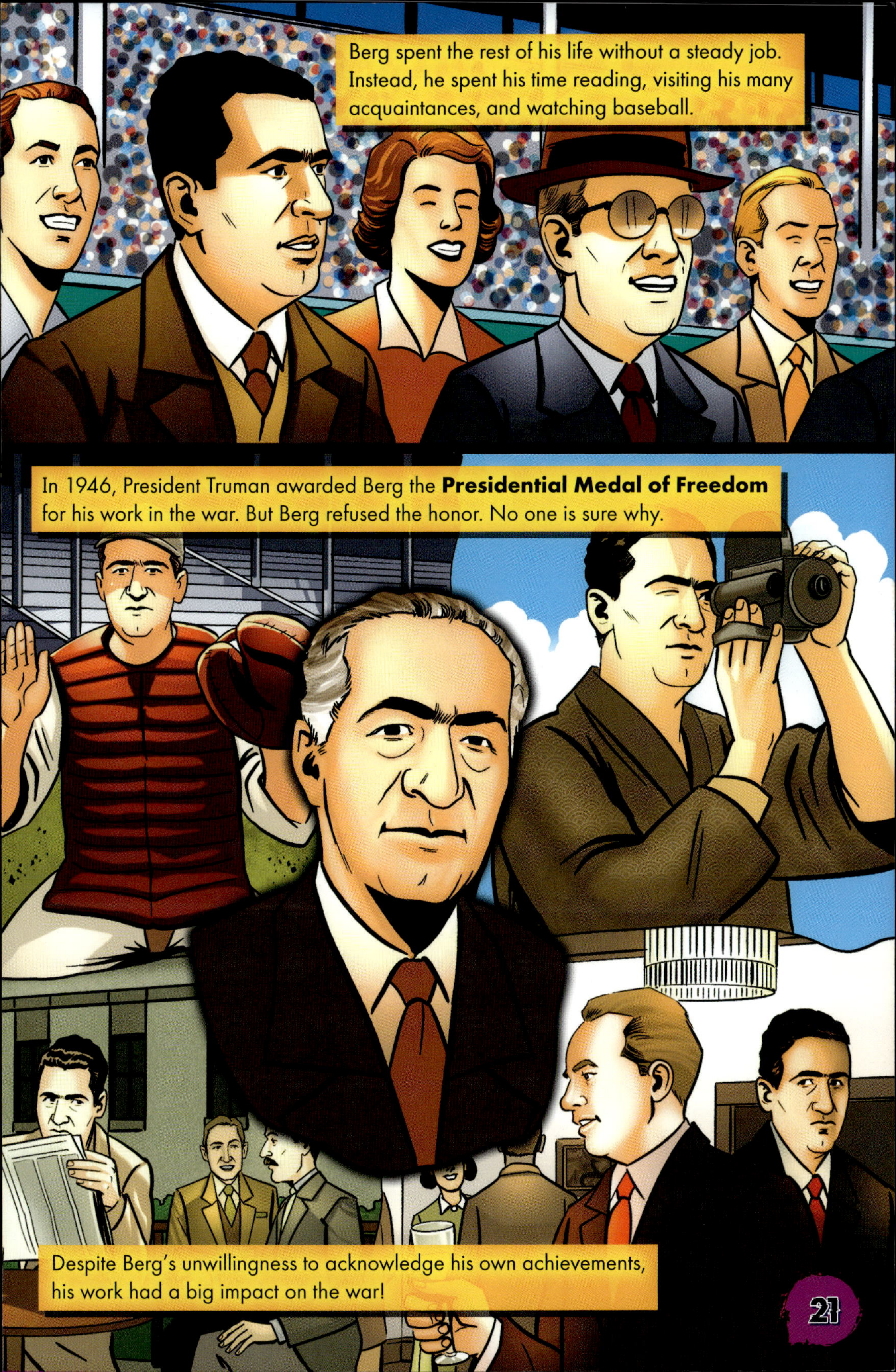
Berg spent the rest of his life without a steady job. Instead, he spent his time reading, visiting his many acquaintances, and watching baseball.
In 1946, President Truman awarded Berg the **Presidential Medal of Freedom** for his work in the war. But Berg refused the honor. No one is sure why.
Despite Berg's unwillingness to acknowledge his own achievements, his work had a big impact on the war!

MORE ABOUT MOE BERG

- **Berg played** for five major league teams during his career. They were the Brooklyn Robins, the Chicago White Sox, the Cleveland Indians, the Washington Senators, and the Boston Red Sox.

- Berg could speak 12 languages at varying levels.

- Berg's information on Germany's atomic bomb was key to the U.S.'s own atomic work. He also convinced scientists, including Edoardo Amaldi, to come to the U.S. for research programs.

- Berg was a baseball fan until he died. His last words were, "How did the Mets do today?"

- Berg's sister accepted the Presidential Medal of Freedom for Berg after his death. It is now in the Baseball Hall of Fame.

MOE BERG TIMELINE

1934 — Moe Berg travels to Japan on a baseball exhibition tour and takes a secret video of Tokyo

December 7, 1941 — Japan bombs Pearl Harbor

July 1942 — Berg shows his film of Tokyo to top U.S. intelligence officers

August 1942 — Berg begins travelling around Latin America

August 1943 — Berg joins the OSS

June 1944 — Berg travels to Italy to speak with Italian physicists

December 1944 — Berg attends a lecture given by Heisenberg in Zürich, Switzerland

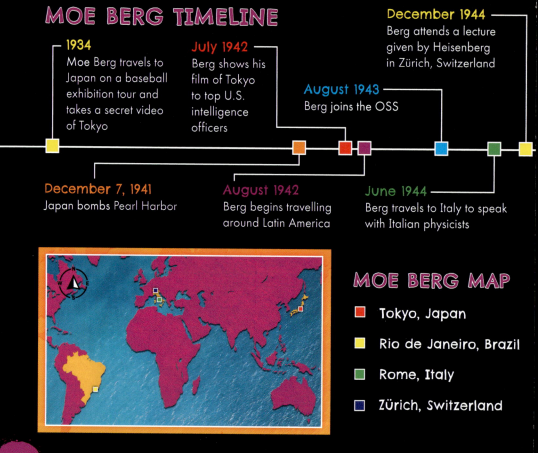

MOE BERG MAP

- ■ Tokyo, Japan
- ■ Rio de Janeiro, Brazil
- ■ Rome, Italy
- ■ Zürich, Switzerland

GLOSSARY

Allies—countries that fought against Germany and other Axis Powers during World War II; Great Britain, the Soviet Union, France, and the United States were Allied Powers.

ambassador—a person who represents one country in another country

atomic bomb—a deadly bomb powered by the energy released when certain atoms are split

classified—kept secret by the government for security

deliberately—on purpose

exhibition—related to competitions played outside of the regular season that are meant to show off a team's skill; exhibition games usually have no impact on a team's rankings.

foreign—related to a country or place outside of one's own country

intelligence—relating to information about an enemy

liberated—freed from the control of a hostile military force

missile—relating to an object used as a weapon that is launched to hit something far away

neutral—not favoring either side in a war

physicist—a scientist who studies physics; physics is a science that deals with matter, energy, heat, light, electricity, motion, and sound.

Presidential Medal of Freedom—the highest non-military award in the United States

scholar—a person who attends a school

Soviet—related to the Soviet Union; the Soviet Union was a country that spanned across eastern Europe and northern Asia from 1922 to 1991.

strategic—of great importance for a certain purpose

surrendered—agreed to stop fighting

theory—related to scientists who come up with explanations for natural occurrences

traits—distinguishing qualities

TO LEARN MORE

AT THE LIBRARY

Cipriano, Jeri. *Moe Berg: Spy Catcher*. Egremont, Mass.: Red Chair Press, 2018.

Monroe, Alex. *World War II*. Minneapolis, Minn.: Bellwether Media, 2024.

Sheinkin, Steve. *Bomb (Graphic Novel): The Race to Build—and Steal—the World's Most Dangerous Weapon*. New York, N.Y.: Roaring Brook Press, 2023.

ON THE WEB

FACTSURFER

Factsurfer.com gives you a safe, fun way to find more information.

1. Go to www.factsurfer.com.
2. Enter "Moe Berg" into the search box and click 🔍.
3. Select your book cover to see a list of related content.

INDEX

Allies, 9, 12
Amaldi, Edoardo, 12, 13
atomic bomb, 10, 11, 12, 14, 15, 16, 18, 19, 20
baseball, 4, 5, 6, 8, 21
Germany, 10, 11, 12, 13, 14, 16, 18, 19, 20
Heisenberg, Werner, 10, 13, 14, 15, 17, 18, 19, 20
historical quotes, 6, 8, 11, 13, 15, 17, 18
Italy, 10, 11, 12, 14

Japan, 6, 7, 8, 20
Latin America, 8, 9
Nazis, 9, 16, 17, 18
Office of Strategic Services, 9, 10, 13, 15, 16, 17, 19, 20
Office of the Coordinator of Inter-American Affairs, 8, 9
Scherrer, Paul, 15, 17, 18, 19
United States, 5, 6, 8, 9, 13, 17, 20
Wick, Gian Carlo, 12, 13
World War II, 8, 9, 18, 19, 20, 21
Zürich, Switzerland, 14, 15, 16, 19